Most parents worry about how they would cope if one of their children were admitted to hospital, and for nearly one million children every year it becomes a reality. Parents are faced with having to comfort and support a child who may not only be sick but in pain, when they themselves are feeling nervous and anxious. Yet it is well known how much parents can contribute to their child's recovery by being there and giving loving support, and this is much easier to do if they know what to expect.

This practical book, written in collaboration with The National Association for the Welfare of Children in Hospital (NAWCH) covers all aspects of a hospital stay, from first admission to convalescence. It offers sensible advice, practical tips and a wealth of information that will enable parents to help their child, and the whole family, to cope with the experience together. It will also contribute to a happy recovery for the sick child.

Acknowledgements

I should like to thank Jan Date of NAWCH for her unfailing and constructive help during the writing of this book and also Dr Michael Williams for sparing the time to show me round the children's wards at Watford General Hospital. I must also thank Sue Reed for allowing me to quote from her son, Christopher's, account of his visit to an Outpatients department. And of course I'd also like to thank Christopher for 'dictating' that account.

M C

NAWCH is grateful to the Nuffield Foundation for their support with the publication of this book.

MARGARET CARTER

You and Your Child in Hospital

Illustrated by Mark Burgess

METHUEN · LONDON

First published in Great Britain 1989
by Methuen Children's Books Ltd
Michelin House, 81 Fulham Road, London SW3 6RB

Photoset by Rowland Phototypesetting Ltd
Bury St Edmunds, Suffolk
Printed in Great Britain by
Cox and Wyman Ltd
Reading, Berks.

British Library Cataloguing in Publication Data

Carter, Margaret
You and your child in hospital.
1. Hospitalisation. Personal adjustment of
children
I. Title
362.1'9892

ISBN 0-416-03052-1

CONTENTS

For convenience and to avoid repetition in this book, the child has been referred to throughout as 'he'. For the same reason the book is addressed to the child's parents and, in particular, the mother since she is the most likely person to be involved. The term however also denotes father, relative or whoever the child's principal carer might be.

PREFACE

'Kiss it better.'

'Cuddle me.'

'Take the pain away.'

'Put a bandage on it.'

How many times have you heard remarks like that from young children? Plasters and bandages, they know, can banish pain – but so, mysteriously, can kisses and cuddles.

Children know about being well and being ill; they know about accidents, bumps, falls and bruises. Watch with what enjoyment they perform operations on Ted, administer pills, listen to heartbeats and give injections. And with what sternness they admonish the doll reluctant to take her medicine: 'Come along now, it will make you better.'

Whether or not they are acting out their fears doesn't really matter for now: what does matter is that from a very early age children seem to know about healing and curing.

They know something else, too. When a child says, 'Kiss it better' he is acknowledging the special power of a trusted adult. He is saying, 'Because I trust you, you can help me.'

That gives the adult two stepping stones towards helping a child who has to go into hospital, because he already understands about curing and about trust.

Your child may never need to go into hospital nor may any child you know, but if it should happen there are many ways to help make the experience less distressing for everyone. The first step is to introduce children to the idea that doctors and hospitals are there to help people get better.

We all want to protect our children. It's one of an adult's strongest instincts. We want to protect them from pain, from unhappiness and from fear and it's difficult to come to terms with the knowledge that we won't be able to do that all their lives and that a stay in hospital could involve some of those experiences – discomfort, apprehension, bewilderment.

Quite illogically, too, we may feel that our child's illness is somehow our fault – as though we'd failed to protect him from suffering. All parents would willingly change places with their children to save them pain; but we can't. What we can do is reduce their apprehension with our informed support.

That support can begin long before any question of illness or hospital treatment might arise: it begins in the attitude to hospital that we are able to instil in the child.

ONE

Hospitals help people get better

Don't wait for a hospital visit to seem likely before you begin to accustom your child to the idea that hospitals are part of everyday life.

When you go out for a walk, or shopping with your child, you no doubt quite naturally point out places of interest, such as the fire station, the park, or the school where one day he will go. You probably point out the school, or the playgroup, without thinking very deeply about it because you are instinctively getting him used to the idea of something that's going to happen in the future; you're preparing him to accept a new experience.

So, in the same way, point out the doctor's surgery, the clinic and the hospital. If there's an ambulance about, so much the better: 'It's a special sort of car where you can lie down and rest if you're not feeling well, and it takes you straight to the hospital so they can make you better quickly.'

It's easier to talk like this when there's no suggestion of a hospital stay because you'll be relaxed about it and the conversation will be quite casual and matter-of-fact.

If he asks questions, answer them honestly but as simply as his age requires.

This conversation took place with a four-year-old:

'Will I ever have to go into hospital?'

'I shouldn't think so, but you might. Daddy did: he hurt his arm playing football and they mended it for him. He couldn't give you swings if his arm hadn't been right.'

'Have you been into hospital?'

'No.'

'Would you like to go?'

'Not unless I had something that had to be put right.'

'If you went into hospital who would look after me?'

'Well, there's Daddy, and Granny, isn't there? But anyway, I'm not going, am I? And if I did, you could come and see me.'

Long pause. 'If you went, I'm coming too.'

'Well, that's settled. And if you went, I'd come too.'

'Yes, that's settled.'

Games and toys help children to understand

All children play 'doctors and nurses' quite naturally and there are plenty of toys and games to help them – doctor's sets with small stethoscopes, thermometers and so on. All these trickle information through to a young child in the same way that his daily life gradually accustoms him to the world he lives in – visiting, playing, talking, being happy, angry or lonely.

There are miniature ward-sets, ambulances, stretchers and all kinds of objects he can play with: the most successful Christmas present I ever made was an apron and headband made from an old white pillow-case, with a 'Red Cross' ribbon on the front of each.

Let him 'take your pulse', give you 'medicine', bandage you up, if it gets that far!

What about visiting a hospital?

If you know a child who's gone into hospital, then mention it to your child and *tell him when the other child is home again*. If

there's an opportunity, take him to visit a child in the children's ward, or even an adult patient, if the circumstances aren't frightening or distressing.

Another opportunity for a child to visit hospital may be to see Mum and a new baby. Although the child will also be coping with the idea of a temporarily absent Mum and a new arrival in the family, a post-natal ward is a reassuringly happy place to visit. There are usually lots of flowers about and a general atmosphere of affection and rejoicing which will convey to a child that a hospital, though it may be strange, can also be an interesting and hopeful place.

And there are books . . .

Look along the library or bookshop shelves and you'll find books for all ages of children about seeing the doctor, the dentist, the optician and so on.

Some refer to specific illnesses or conditions, others are more general. It is wise to vet the books yourself before introducing them to your child because you know him best and what some children find disturbing, others will take in their stride.

Don't provide a steady diet of 'going into hospital' books – that would make the most trusting child a bit suspicious – but you can always include one or two among the general books.

NAWCH (National Association for the Welfare of Children in Hospital) publish a list of books for children dealing with visiting hospital, seeing the doctor and many allied subjects. Some of these are very simple stories, others more detailed. A complete list is available from NAWCH, (address on page 84) on receipt of a stamped self-addressed envelope, but the following short list is of books specially recommended for young children.

Books for the under fives

Going into Hospital; Althea (Dinosaur). Excellent for preparing children for planned admission: designed to allay fears and answer questions in advance. Deals with separation, care of personal possessions, hospital routines and many types of treatment.

Going to Hospital; Camilla Jessel (Methuen). Jamie has asthma and is admitted to hospital. Attractive photographs of admission procedures, medical examination and X rays are shown.

Ruth goes to Hospital; *Lucy loses her tonsils*; Nigel Snell (Hamish Hamilton). Ruth cuts her leg and has stitches and an X-ray. In *Lucy loses her tonsils* – the details of admission and operation-day procedures are good.

For fives and upwards

Jane has asthma; Nigel Snell (Hamish Hamilton). Jane has tests in Outpatients: illustrations are attractive and she responds quickly to treatment.

Talkabout going to hospital; Pauline Wells (Ladybird). Lots of details and pictures about children in hospital.

Linda goes to hospital; Barrie Wade (A & C Black). Eight year old Linda has her tonsils out. Ideal for preparing a child for hospital.

Paul in Hospital; Camilla Jessel (Methuen). Paul has blood poisoning following an unwashed cut. The story follows his

in-patient treatment with lots of detail of ward routine and medical procedures. Realistic photographs – a good read for junior-aged children.

Going to the Hospital; Anne Civardi and Stephen Cartwright (Usborne). Ben has earache and goes into hospital to have an operation. Everything about this book – the text and the illustrations – is wholly reassuring and informative. Suitable for both pre-school and infant children.

The number of books on these subjects is always being increased, so it's a matter of looking through the shelves and choosing a book to suit your child. Some titles deal with specific illnesses or conditions – *Johnny gets some glasses*, *Peter gets a Hearing Aid*, for instance. The books by Althea cover a wide range of different conditions.

There's no doubt that preparing a child in this way is enormously helpful if he has to face the situation himself. All these suggestions – talking, playing, looking at books – help create the climate for a child in which he can understand what hospitals are for, even though he may never be a patient.

TWO

Learning to separate

A very young child doesn't see himself as separate from his most familiar adult – usually his mother. It's only gradually that he comes to realise that he's a separate person, and so is she. If she's out of sight, she'll come back. (Playing Peepo round a door is one of the ways we begin to teach babies about coming and going).

Slowly, a baby also learns that if he goes somewhere, when he returns, his mother will be there. And if she's not *here* – then she's somewhere else.

A young child in hospital needs the support and comfort of his mother (or another familiar adult) but, if he is used to the idea that Mum does occasionally go shopping on her own while he stays for an hour or two with Granny or Dad, it will be easier for him to accept that for very short periods while he's in hospital it's 'safe' to let Mum out of his sight while she goes out for a walk, or a meal, or a short break. He can be sure that she'll always come back.

It might be possible – and it will certainly help share the strain – to arrange for another relative or friend to come in and visit for a short while while Mum has a break. Children have a different relationship with other people, just as adults do, and it's good for them to have a change of company. Dads, grannies, grandpas, uncles, aunts and friends all bring their own special atmosphere and interest which will be stimulating for a child and help to relieve what could become a rather tedious time for the parent.

But you could be wasting your time if . . .

All this building of confidence and knowledge could be a waste of time if, by lowered voices, half-finished sentences,

nods, hints and enigmatic remarks meant to be above the child's understanding, we give the impression that actually pretty nasty things go on in hospital.

Any child soon catches on to the fact that what we're saying to *him* is very different from what we're saying to other people. And there's no surer way to destroy a child's trust in us.

And it goes without saying that we should never use the threat of hospital as a punishment, or say something like, 'Mummy will end up in hospital if you don't stop worrying her.'

Don't also underestimate a child's understanding . . .

We underestimate alarmingly when it comes to assessing a child's understanding. Just because they haven't the vocabulary to express themselves it doesn't mean that children aren't aware of the threats and unspoken anxiety in the atmosphere. Their radar is faultless in picking up what *isn't* being said.

If you think that is perhaps an exaggeration, read this account of a hospital visit. It was 'dictated' to his mother by a little boy under four years of age. At the age of three and a half he had his adenoids taken out and grommets fitted in each ear but it was later decided that further tests would be needed. He was already used to such tests and appointments and had found them – at the local Children's Centre and hospital – interesting and not at all alarming. This appointment, however, was at a different hospital. This is how Christopher describes the visit.

'This hospital didn't have any toys or books or any children's chairs. We had to sit in a straight line in a long white tunnel.* Luckily my mum had brought some books and toys for my sister and me. The trouble is there was nowhere to play. If we sat on the floor we got in the way and you can't play properly sitting on a chair. We had to wait a long time and we got bored.

'The doctor didn't talk to me, only to my mum. Although he talked to her he didn't look at her. He said I had to have some more tests and then we had to wait another very long time.

'I told my mum I didn't want any more tests but she said I had to, so I had to.

'I couldn't understand the testing lady† and in her room there were no windows or pictures. I could only see the top of her head over the testing boxes on her table. I had to say "one" when I heard a noise in my left ear and "two" when I heard a noise in my right ear. Although I know left and right I kept doing it wrong and I got hot and cross. I said I wouldn't do any more tests. Mum and the lady were looking a bit cross.

'Then she said, "Can you hear this?" but in the end I just nodded when she nodded and shook my head when she shook hers because I didn't want everyone to be cross.

'The lady said my mother and sister should wait outside and I started to cry. Mum said she was staying so I wasn't to cry.

'The lady said she gave up. Mum said something very quietly

*waiting room was a corridor

†she had a foreign accent – and the little boy was already hard of hearing.

but I don't know what she said. We waited in the tunnel again.

'The doctor said I had to have more grommets put in and while they were doing that they'd take my tonsils out. My mum looked surprised and said I hadn't had any trouble with my tonsils but the doctor said it would save time later.

'My mum was very quiet in the car going home. I asked her if she was cross and she said yes, she was, but not with me.'

Wouldn't you love to know what 'mum said very quietly'!

A second opinion later confirmed that it was quite unnecessary to take out the little boy's tonsils.

But what a lot there is to be learnt from that account: the child's awareness of the atmosphere: his shrewdness – 'the doctor didn't speak to me and didn't look at my mum': the unfortunate foreign accent: the discomfort of the surroundings – the white tunnel, the lack of chairs or play space, the complete idiocy of asking a small harrassed boy to distinguish between left and right: and the 'threat' of having to have his tonsils out. How easily all that could have been avoided.

But what also comes over just as strongly is the wonderful security the child felt because his mother was there. *'I said I didn't want to do any more tests but mum said I had to, so I had to!'* Then there's the assurance from mum that *'she was staying so I wasn't to cry.'* And the final triumphant *'Mum said she was cross, but not with me.'*

Four-year-old Christopher put into his one account more information about how hospitals should be run, how children treated, and how doctors trained than could be achieved by a library full of text books.

He has also shown once and for all that even a young child can cope with potentially disturbing experiences if a familiar and trusted adult is there to support him.

THREE

Sick children need their parents

It's hardly a new idea that sick children need their parents. This was written in 1772: *'If you take a sick child from its parent you break its heart immediately.'*

So how did it ever come about that sick children – even a few years ago – should be handed over to hospitals to be made well and then returned to their parents without the parents being involved at all in their care? Visiting was strictly limited.

A paediatrician, Dr Hugh Jolly, recalled that, as a young houseman in the 1940s coming on duty at a children's hospital on a Sunday afternoon, he could hear the children crying *three streets away* as the weekly visiting hour came to an end.

Home and hospital were rigidly separated and parents were expected to keep well out of the way and let the 'professionals' get on with their jobs.

But one of the reasons for this separation is, interestingly enough, because nursing and treatment were getting so much better. Previous generations took it for granted that sick children would be nursed at home but, as medical knowledge increased, doctors began to realise that children are not 'miniature adults' but suffer from illnesses and conditions different from grown-ups.

They began to specialise in children's ailments and gradually cures became routine for illnesses that would previously have been fatal. It must have been an exciting time – and perhaps because the advances being made were so dramatic, it was thought that only 'professionals' and hospitals could bring them about.

It took some time for two more aspects of child illness to be recognised. Today we take them for granted but only thirty or so years ago they were quite revolutionary, at least to the 'professionals' if not to parents.

In the first place it was recognised that parents weren't just people who got in the way of the trained hospital staff: they were people who – with a little basic training – could be of immense help to the whole routine of caring for sick children.

Secondly, it was realised just how much children suffered if they were separated from their parents and how much the presence and support of their parents could help their recovery.

An unhappy child takes longer to get well than a child who is nurtured by the support of those he loves and trusts

However kind hospital staff are to a child, they are strangers. It's bad enough for an adult to have to go into hospital but it's a lot worse for a child who can't ask the right questions, know when he's coming home, or even demand a second opinion!

Children thrive on affection and security – and if that's true when they're well it must apply a great deal more when they're ill.

Today it's taken for granted that children in hospital should have their parents with them for as long as the parents can manage; that there should be unrestricted visiting, and facilities for parents to stay overnight.

They are not regarded as nuisances who get in the way of the staff; they are regarded as essential to the recovery of their children. (There is more about parents and hospitals in chapter seven.)

Parents need their children

Caring for their children is one way that parents express their love. When their child is ill they need to express that love even more. It is natural to want to be with them. Children and parents need each other – when they're well and when they're ill. Parents are essential members of the team of people caring for their sick child.

It's worth remembering, too, that all 'punishment' is based

on the withdrawal of love or approval. The person is 'banished' – perhaps from our interest, affection or from our physical presence. A child left in hospital without frequent visiting or support from those he knows and cares for most will feel banished. So he will also feel punished and think he has done something wrong to merit this treatment.

It's significant that even adults, talking of themselves or others who have suffered misfortune or illness, often say, 'Why should it happen to *me*/him? I've/he's always been so *good*!' What they are saying without realising it, is that they are thinking of the misfortune as a punishment – unjustified maybe, but still a retribution which should only be given to those who have done wrong.

FOUR

Going into hospital

If your child has to go to hospital it will be as one of the following:

1. Outpatient
2. Planned admission
3. Emergency

Outpatient

This will be because your doctor has referred you to the hospital for a second opinion or tests or perhaps an X-ray. He's using the better facilities and equipment of a hospital to confirm or change his treatment or diagnosis.

The child won't be expected to stay in overnight (see page 23). You *must* have an appointment – arranged through your doctor – you can't just turn up (unless it's an emergency when you'll go straight to the Accident and Emergency Department – see page 32). Your doctor may ask you to take with you a letter of introduction and explanation of your child's situation or he may send it separately.

The hospital staff will try to see you at the fixed time of your appointment but you may have to wait if they've been delayed by a previous patient who has needed longer consultations than they'd planned for.

The hospital may or may not have a separate waiting room for children. In any case take a few books with you for your child and perhaps his favourite toy or cuddly. No harm in taking Ted with a bandage if your child is young enough.

If you have another child you might consider taking him along, too, as that would get him used to the idea of going into a hospital. But that depends to a large extent on his age: a baby can

take up so much of your attention that it wouldn't be fair on the child who is the reason for the visit and who needs your attention for himself. You could find yourself distracted and occupied just in 'keeping them quiet' unless a friend or relation can come along with you to help with the children and give you some support.

An older child, however, can be a help in amusing a younger one or even helping him to co-operate.

Before you go, jot down any questions you'd like to ask – it's easy to forget them in the general business of being seen.

If your child has to undress, you do it for him and if possible hold him for his examination. Most doctors will expect you to do this and will probably show you the best way to hold the child for an examination.

There may be students with the doctor when your child is being examined. You have the right to refuse to have them but it is the way they learn to become doctors. Unless they are upsetting the child it's best to accept their presence as being necessary.

If the doctor wants to talk to you about your child's condition, decide before you go whether you want it to be in front of the child. It could upset him more to be 'sent outside' but an older child could help by taking him 'for a walk' or a nurse might do so.

If an X-ray is needed, ask if you can go with him to the room (see page 32), wait with him and bring him back to the consulting room.

It is rare that a child has to stay in as a result of an outpatient's appointment. If he does so, it is best to take the child home first, collect familiar clothes and toys, and then return to the hospital. If possible, stay with him overnight. This way, he won't think that any other visit to Outpatients is automatically going to mean staying in.

Hospitals vary in their facilities so ask your doctor if the one he's sending you to has a special children's outpatients with playroom and toys. If not, ring your local NAWCH branch and find out if any others do.

Planned admission

This is when you've known for some time that your child has a condition or ailment which will need hospital treatment in the future. That could range from having his tonsils or his adenoids out, having a grommet inserted, or, more long term, the correction of some disorder or malfunction.

It is easier to prepare a child for a planned admission because you'll have time to 'make the climate' in which he accepts that a hospital stay is something that is going to happen in the future.

It's also likely that whatever the condition is that needs treatment, it will be obvious to him and perhaps be causing discomfort. He will thus see the forthcoming stay in hospital as bringing cure and relief.

How much or how little you can prepare your child depends on his age and level of understanding. It's important not to overdo the explanation. This could be a temptation if you're concerned about the event yourself and some of that spills over into too many details.

If the child asks a question that you cannot answer accurately, don't improvise but tell him you will ask the doctor or nurse at the hospital. It is far better to wait for the correct answer than have things happen to the child that do not tally with your own explanation.

Below the age of two you can't really explain very much beyond the occasional cheerful assurance that 'some day' he'll visit the hospital to make – whatever it is – better. Such a reference should always end with 'Mummy will come too' or 'Mummy will be there' or 'Daddy will come'. If he is old enough to ask if, say, teddy can come too, then of course you'll assure him that teddy will also be there. (Later, there could be a chance to get teddy's case packed and his pyjamas ready, and so on).

But don't begin with even minor explanations too soon. Time means nothing to a young child – today, tomorrow, next week are all grown-up mysteries. The best approach is to make this matter-of-fact climate in which the child accepts the inevitable that will happen 'some time'.

Well before his admission find out what arrangements for children the hospital makes. Is there a playroom? What facilities are there for you to stay overnight? Will you need to take, for example, a sleeping bag? Will you be allowed to stay with your child for the pre-med, if used, before the operation? How long will he be there?

A few hospitals run a club where children who are to be admitted in the future go along for an hour or two in the atmosphere of a playgroup so that they can get used to the surroundings – but these are few and far between. Many hospitals produce leaflets with details about their arrangements and some will suggest that you visit with your child so you can see things for yourself. The more you know about the hospital the more at ease you'll be – and that will be passed on as reassurance to your child. But, once again, don't begin all this preparation too soon or make it too obvious.

If you feel you don't know enough about what's going to happen you could telephone either the Ward Sister or the Paediatric Nursing Officer. The latter in some hospitals may be called the Nurse Manager, Paediatrics, or Senior Nurse, Paediatrics.

Medical questions should be addressed to a doctor. For general or 'informal' advice talk to your GP or Health Visitor.

When you know the date for admission tell your child – but only a few days before. Reinforce that you'll be there, that you will stay with him (if you are) and that he will be visited, perhaps by Daddy, Granny or other brothers and sisters, and that he will soon be coming home.

He will probably like to help with getting his case packed – and yours, too, if you're staying.

You'll know which special things to put in his case but here's a list of basics.

Day clothes and shoes
Pyjamas or nightclothes
Dressing gown and slippers
Brush, comb, toilet things

Favourite toy – teddy or whatever. (Don't worry if they're shabby: they are what he is used to and that's what matters).
Small toys that are right for his age
Any cup or feeder, spoon etc. he's used to
Books
Colouring book and crayons or pencils.

Be a bit wary about including toys that could make a bit of a mess. Most nurses are understanding about spills on the bedclothes when children are bedbound but at first a child can so easily be upset even by 'pretend' crossness and it can make for a lot of unhappiness and anxiety. The chances are there'll be plenty of opportunities for 'messy play' later.

In your own case, as well as your nightclothes and toilet things, it's a good idea to pack magazines or a book and perhaps your knitting or mending. Waiting in hospital or sitting with a young child can be very boring, particularly when – as often happens – they get so absorbed in playing with the other children that they ignore you!

Depending on what overnight accommodation is provided by the hospital you might need to take a sleeping bag or rug.

It's also sensible to take a few coffee or tea bags, a thermos flask and a small supply of 'emergency rations' such as a packet of biscuits or an apple or two. There may not be canteen facilities, or they may have opening hours which don't fit in with your appetite, and if there's no restaurant or café near the hospital you could get decidedly hungry.

Don't forget the invaluable supply of small change for telephone calls as well as the telephone numbers of those you'll want to keep in touch with – relatives, friends and neighbours. Or, now that phone-card call boxes are more usual, it might be worth buying a phone-card – at least you won't be cut off by the pips!

When you get to the hospital, a sister or nurse on the children's ward will be almost sure to greet your child by name and introduce herself to you both.

She'll show you which bed is his and also where to find the bathroom, lavatory and so on.

She may ask that your child is undressed and put into bed. If so, you do it for him, fold his clothes, put them in his locker and say you'll leave them there until he's been made better and will need them to wear when he comes home again.

A child's clothes are very important to him: he regards them as part of himself and to take them away with you conveys to him even more strongly that he is being 'abandoned'. If there really is no room to leave them all – winter overcoat or whatever – then leave some and explain why you're taking some away. Don't try to hide things like that from him.

Having one's own clothes gives dignity and self-respect. If your child doesn't have to get into bed straightaway, then ask a nurse or sister if you can take him for a walk round the hospital or into the playroom or out into the garden.

If you have to leave the child at this stage, try not to go off in too much of a hurry: stay and read a story or play a game and then, when you do go, explain exactly when you'll be back and why you're going – to get the other children's tea, or to shop, or whatever.

If Daddy or another relative is coming in, tell the child when he'll be coming – and keep faith with him.

If he cries, try not to get too upset yourself and never – just because you are upset – try to sneak away when he's not looking. All children would rather know that you're going but have your promise that you'll return, than have you deceive them and break their trust in you.

You could leave something of yours with the child as a reassurance, such as a glove or hanky.

Before you go, tell the nurse or ward sister when you'll be back.

Some parents tie a note on the bed saying when they will be back or who else will be coming, and when. This helps ward staff to reassure the child and in a busy ward with lots of staff, that kind of information at hand can be invaluable.

If your child has any special words for going to the lavatory, wanting a drink or so on, then explain these to the staff.

And always come back when you said you would.

Emergency admission

Emergency admissions are likely to be a lot more upsetting for everyone involved because of the suddenness – and maybe the potential danger – of what has happened, whether it's an

accident or the sudden flare up of an illness. One moment life is normal, the next moment – confusion.

However mistaken they may be, children expect their parents to be in control and to know what to do, so, for their sakes as well as your own, try to keep calm. Panic is catching and your child may be frightened enough anyway without having to cope with an atmosphere of hysteria and bewilderment.

If you're faced with an illness or condition, such as appendicitis or a sudden bad attack of asthma, you'll almost certainly have already been in touch with your doctor and he or she will have told you what to do if the condition worsens. If she hasn't, then ask her.

The questions you might ask

1. Is this condition likely to worsen suddenly?
2. If so, what emergency steps should I take?
3. Should I ring you or the hospital first?
4. Is there a particular ward I should ring?
5. Supposing I can't get through to the hospital?
6. Is it best to ring for an ambulance or take the child myself (supposing you have your own transport)?
7. Should the child be placed in a particular position/given drinks/something to eat etc.?

(This could be important if there's the likelihood of an emergency operation. Positioning a child correctly, whether upright, lying flat, on his side etc., could help ease pain.)

You will obviously go with your child in the ambulance or whatever transport you have, so get together his nightclothes and a favourite toy or cuddly in case there's an overnight stay involved. You may also need to take your own nightclothes.

FIVE

Emergencies caused by accidents

If an emergency is caused through an accident then the chances are you'll be on your own or, hopefully, with friends but without immediate medical advice to hand.

Being prepared for smaller emergencies can help if you have to cope with a greater one, and you'll find a section on First Aid on pages 79–83. While you're dealing as best you can with the emergency you'll also need to get help. This list will be invaluable for you, or anyone with you, if you fill in the details and keep the book in a fixed place. If it is a library book, or if you prefer, copy out the details and stick them on your First Aid Box or Noticeboard.

Nearest telephone
(if you haven't one at home) ....

The telephone number of:
Your doctor ....
Local hospital ....
Neighbours who might help 1 ....
2 ....
Relatives who should know of your whereabouts 1 ....
2 ....

Children's schools ....
Workplace/office ....
Anyone else who might help in an emergency ....

Having taken what emergency steps you can and enlisted help, your main concern is to keep the child as quiet and comfortable as possible. You may also be able to pick up nightclothes and a toy as mentioned on page 25.

If you have to leave home suddenly, the chances are you'll be so concerned with dealing with the accident itself that ordinary home matters may be forgotten, so here are some reminders.

1. *Are there other children at school you must make arrangements for?* – bringing them home, taking them in for an hour or two, giving them a meal etc.?
2. *Have you turned off everything* – fires, cooking stoves, washing machines, iron etc.? Do you need to put a fireguard up?
3. *Have you locked all outside doors?*

Some of these details may seem far-removed from actually dealing with getting your child into hospital and helping him over the hurdle, but often the difficulties of an emergency are as much concerned with the home as with getting medical attention.

Someone alone at home with young children is particularly vulnerable if there's a crisis and nothing is more necessary or reassuring than knowing there's a neighbour you can call on if, say, an older child has to be let in, an animal fed, the backdoor locked or the washing machine turned off.

Getting to hospital

Ambulance attendants are invariably kind, reassuring and knowledgeable. They'll know what to do – and you'll immediately feel better as soon as they arrive. It may help your child if he already knows what an ambulance looks like, inside and outside.

On arrival at hospital

The ambulance attendants will know which entrance to take you to. That isn't as silly as it sounds. Big hospitals have so many

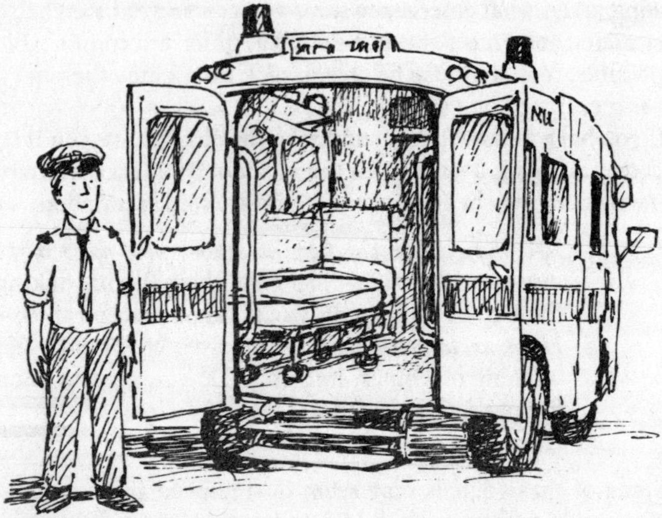

entrances that, if you're driving yourself, you may find yourself going round in circles before you find the right one. One local hospital – world-famous for specialist treatments as well as being a general hospital – has at least ten entrances and the buildings are spread over many acres. Does it sound ghoulish, or wise, to suggest that if you're near your own local hospital, you have a look to see which is the Accident and Emergency Entrance? It could save many minutes and much worry.

You'll be seen in the Accident and Emergency Department. The chances are that there'll be a waiting room with people sitting around. If yours is a real emergency you should be seen straight away in a side cubicle.

Tests may be necessary, or perhaps an X-ray to see if bones are broken. If an operation is needed, ask if you can carry your child yourself to the pre-med or anaesthetic room. It's only natural that you'll be worried, shocked and tense and the staff will understand that, but try to be very calm and co-operative so you'll be seen as a help, not a hindrance. Your child will be needing you more than anyone else and you won't be helping him if you're hysterical, argumentative or in a dead faint on the floor.

Some common questions, and answers

Do injections hurt?
Not if you go 'floppy'.

Do drip feeds hurt?
Only the needleprick as they go in.

Does it hurt to have stitches?
Only the local anaesthetic prick – and then there's no hurt at all.

Does it hurt to have stitches out?
No.

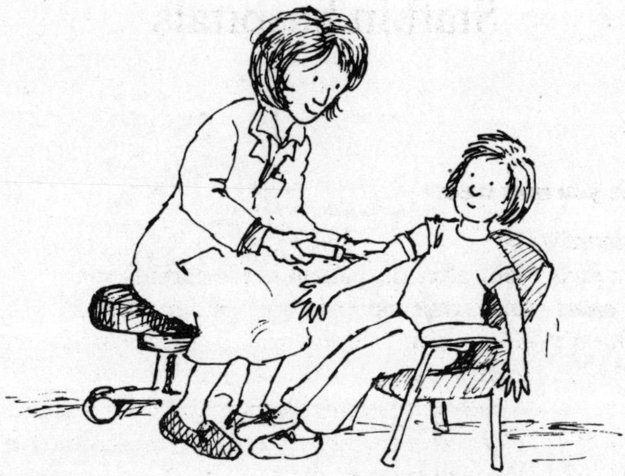

About accidents

The Child Accident Prevention Trust produces a free booklet *Keep Them Safe*, available through your Health Education Unit. It's full of information about safety equipment.

Child car restraints for very young babies are quite expensive. Some areas have initiated a 'loan' scheme whereby you can borrow the restraints through the maternity departments of the local hospitals. It's worth asking if there's such a scheme in your district.

A smoke detector which costs just about £10 with a battery that lasts a year has significantly reduced the death rate among children. There are details in *Keep Them Safe*.

SIX

Staff in hospitals

People you may meet

Ambulance attendants – look after the patient in the ambulance.

Porters – may wheel him to a ward or department.

Doctors – *Consultant Paediatrician*, specialist in child care.

Consultant Surgeon, if an operation is needed.

Consultant Physician – may be responsible for the medical treatment.

The Consultant Paediatrician is likely to be responsible for all the care of your child, but under him will be:

Casualty Officer, if you go to the Accident and Emergency Department.

Registrar and Houseman, responsible for the day to day care of patients.

Medical students may be present – if they worry your child you can ask for them not to be there. (see page 22)

Nurses – *Ward Sisters*, (or *Charge Nurses* if they are male) responsible for the ward.
Staff Nurses, qualified nurses who work under the Ward Sister.
Registered Sick Children's Nurses (see page 43) who have additional qualifications for the care of sick children.
Nursery Nurses who are trained in simple nursing techniques and the care of young children – their diet, needs, toilet training, the value of play, etc. but have not taken a full medical training.
Student and Auxiliary nurses may also be in the ward to assist more senior staff.

Other staff – *Social Workers*
Laboratory technicians
Physiotherapists (help with special exercises)
Playworkers, organise playrooms, supervise play
Radiographers who take X rays

And of course there's a whole army of specialists whom you may meet if your child's condition needs it – *speech therapists*, *teachers*, (if your child is old enough to have lessons or is staying for some time), *dieticians* and so on.

Many hospital staff wear name badges and in some hospitals parents are given them too. NAWCH makes a badge saying 'I am staying with . . .' to help staff match parents to patients.

The chaplain

All hospitals have chaplains for different denominations. Usually they pay regular calls but can always be asked to visit specially if you want to see them.

Even if you are not in the habit of regular church-going, there is no need to feel diffident about talking to a chaplain or asking his assistance. They are invariably knowledgeable and supportive.

If you'd like to talk to a priest or clergyman, ask the Ward Sister or Social Worker to put you in touch.

SEVEN

Parent power

Nowadays hospitals accept that parents should have unrestricted visiting to their children and that they should be allowed to sleep in the hospital if they wish. But acknowledging this was much more of a breakthrough than we realise today because it recognised that curing may not be only a matter of physical treatment: the psychological state of the child also contributed to his recovery.

It was a return to a truth we had probably always known in our hearts but now it was formalised and being acted upon. Expressions like 'treat the whole child', 'study the whole family', 'look at the background' began to be used. The state of 'not being well' was being studied with regard to the illness, the child, the surroundings – social, emotional, and physical.

When in the 1940's psychologists and doctors began to study the effects on a young child of separation from his parents (and at that time very few mothers went out to work full-time) they recorded that the young child 'abandoned' in hospital went through three stages.

At first he cried and protested at being left: next he seemed to give up hope and become apathetic: the third stage was indifference to the parent who, he believed, had left him, (usually the mother). At visiting time he ignored her although he might react almost normally to others less close – father perhaps, or grandmother. His faith and trust in his closest and dearest had been destroyed.

Although it may be difficult and painful sometimes for parents to be with their child in hospital – particularly if he has to undergo distressing treatment – the child knows he has not been abandoned.

Many paediatricians were years ahead of the times in realising the vital part parents could play in their child's recovery. Unrestricted visiting was the order of the day in Newcastle over forty years ago and Dr Hugh Jolly's first action when he became consultant paediatrician in Devonshire in the 1950's was to put up the notice 'Parents welcome at all times'.

What to expect in hospital

Today about 95% of all hospitals in Britain accept as a matter of course that parents should stay if they are able to, but however much goodwill there is, the accommodation provided can vary a great deal because, obviously, not all hospitals have the same facilities. This may be particularly noticeable in older buildings, whereas most new hospitals are now providing parents' units.

So, 'staying overnight' can vary from a put-you-up bed next to your child's bed, to a separate room, or a parents' flat with its own bathroom, kitchen and rest room.

Young children need their parents close at hand, or in sight in case they wake in the night and want them: older children can cope with parents in the building, in a parent unit, or perhaps with landladies in accommodation reasonably close.

As well as the sleeping arrangements, facilities for washing, eating and bathing can all vary: you could find yourself eating in the canteen, cooking your own food in a kitchen, or going out to shop or eat.

How to 'behave'!

Although you have the 'right' to stay with your child you may find you're not invited to do so, nor particularly encouraged, so it may be that you will have to ask. Many parents are diffident about this: it's very easy to be over-awed by the atmosphere, particularly as you'll be anxious enough about your child anyway.

There's an instinct not to 'be any trouble' but it's best to say quite calmly that you want to stay and take it for granted, by your attitude, that you will be expected to do so.

Real 'anti-feeling' towards parents today is rare, thanks to years of pioneering by NAWCH and through the individual efforts of concerned adults – parents and professionals. If there

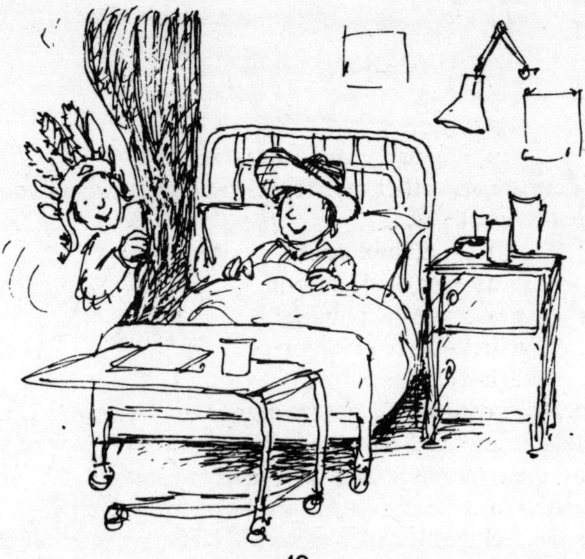

should be queries about your staying, then your best plan is to contact your local NAWCH branch who are very used to negotiating tactfully and will almost certainly be able to advise you without making any upsetting atmospheres.

If you yourself can't stay, perhaps another relative whom the child knows and trusts can do so, or can at least take it in turns with you so that you're able to carry on with other commitments. Often an older brother or sister is a very good substitute – they can bring a companionable 'playmate' feeling to the sick child, and they're often a lot more fun than a parent!

The hospital staff will know you are worried and anxious and will do their best to help – on the other hand not all parents are models of co-operation, tact and sense, any more than all nurses are. So it could be a question of keeping a low profile for a while until you've understood the routine of the ward and then doing your best to fit in and help.

How you help depends on your child's illness and the attitude of the staff. There are some obvious ways:

help in the playroom
playing games, stories
help with making beds
serving meals and feeding
washing
dressing
companionship and general interest

There are also other more specialised tasks where you could be involved such as:

measuring fluid intake
measuring urine output
measuring food intake
giving pills or medicine,
taking temperatures

Ideally, hospitals should make parents feel needed, valued, intelligent and helpful – and also entitled to all information about their child's illness and the procedures that may be necessary to cope with it. It could be up to parents to make hospitals feel that way about them! Which is not to say that the

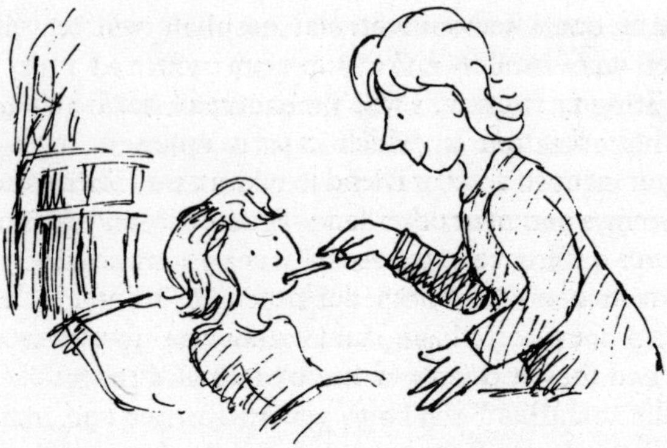

attitude of the staff doesn't help too . . . Nottingham's children's unit, for instance, produces a brochure of welcome and encouragement for parents.

Their idea is to make parents feel AT HOME IN HOSPITAL. There's a question and answer section, lots of information in straightforward language and a pocket in which a leaflet giving details of the particular ward to which the child is to be admitted, is inserted. The pictures are just right too – amusing and reassuring as well as bringing the points home.

Parents help a sick child just by 'being there'

All the same it can be pretty boring to spend hours in a hospital, particularly if the child is asleep or, just as likely, having a riotous time in the playroom and ignoring you completely.

Keep up your own morale in all the ways you can. That can mean going out for walks, shopping or even short visits. Your child will be used to that routine from home and will accept that it's to be expected.

Many children's wards now have pay phones available so children can ring their parents when they want to. And parents, too, can ring for a chat if they can't visit. Older children can be given change or a phone card.

If you have other children at home it may not be so easy to stay overnight but a few enlightened hospitals will let the other children stay as well by making up extra beds in a Family Room.

For varying reasons, some parents may not be able to stay with their children in which case it might be possible for grandparent or relative or friend to take a turn. There's no doubt that having a parent or other familiar adult around does make an enormous difference to the security of a young child.

From about eight months, babies tend to become rather more insecure – they like to have Mum within eyesight all the time. By about two they can cope with occasional absences since they know by then that Mum can, and will, come back – that she exists elsewhere even though they can't see her. A five year old, however, misses Mum of course, but also misses places and routines – his own home, his own bed, familiar china and so on.

All hospitals try to get children home as soon as possible. Investigations which used to entail a stay of a few days can now be accomplished in a day and treatments such as circumcision, mending hernias, and putting on or taking off plaster casts increasingly come under the heading of Day Surgery.

Ideally, children in hospital should be cared for by Registered Sick Children's Nurses – that is, nurses who have qualified in general nursing and then taken further specialised training in nursing sick children.

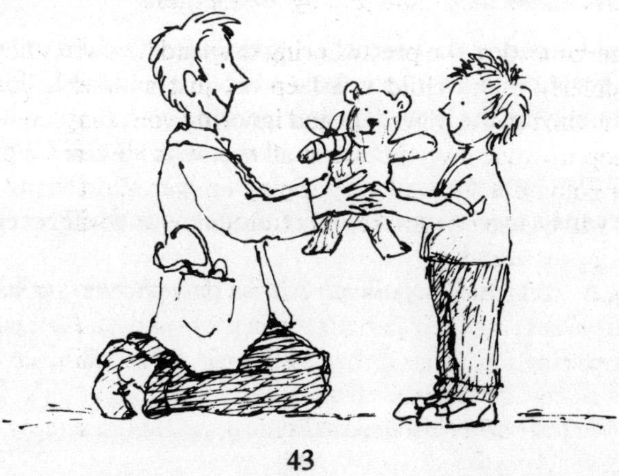

This further training is intensive and wide-ranging. It focusses not only on health but also on child development and the emotional, mental, social and physical needs of children. It reflects the emphasis on thinking of a child as part of his background and family relationships. RSC Nurses are also trained in communicating with families and working with them as partners.

Quite often the sister in charge of a children's ward, or the staff nurse, will have this extra qualification although the rest of her staff may not.

The things people say . . . that are worth thinking about

'You can see I'm a children's doctor, can't you? My trousers have baggy knees and the toes of my shoes are scuffed . . . it's all this kneeling down for eye-to-eye contact . . .'

(*A Paediatrician*)

'If you don't stop running about, I'll get that nurse to give you an injection . . .'

(*Mother in Outpatients to two year old*)

'Listen and you'll hear.'

(*Advice to medical staff*)

'A child is part of his parent: you cannot treat a child unless you treat his parents. In a household where there is a sick child, the parent may be the most damaged person.'

(*A speaker at a NAWCH Conference*)

'Everyone's nice to me but you're the only one who ever cuddles me.'

(*A child, appallingly scarred through burns, to his nurse*)

EIGHT

Facing pain

'Look at all these children suffering! What is God thinking about to let it happen?'

That was said, not by a middle-aged philosopher, but a nine-year-old looking round the children's ward . . . His faith was being severely tested.

Building a child's confidence is very different from false reassurance. Assurances that 'it won't hurt' when you know that treatment may do so, will cause him a lot more suffering; he won't be prepared for discomfort and his trust in you will have been destroyed.

It's essential to be truthful although naturally you explain only to the degree of the child's understanding.

Some parents feel that they'll be so distressed at staying with their children during painful treatment that it will upset their children even more than if they'd not been there.

A good rule of thumb to help us judge is the saying 'put the child in the centre'. What will help *him* most? If you know that it will help him most to have you there, then that's your answer.

It used to be said, in the days before unrestricted visiting, that children cried more when their parents were there. This was taken as a reason for excluding parents. Now we realise that the silent child, the 'brave' child is not suffering less – he may be suffering more but he has sunk into an apathy where he cannot even relieve his feelings in tears.

Reactions to pain

When a number of children were questioned about their reactions to being in hospital, those over ten said when they were afraid they became quiet. Younger children cried more but said they wanted parents with them to explain what was happening.

'It will hurt for about a minute – while we count to 3 . . . 4 . . . 5'

It's one of the most difficult areas to judge – just how much can you explain to a child, and how much prepare them for treatment – but a NAWCH research team found that, overwhelmingly, children did want to be told what was going to happen.

Children – even very young children – long for explanations: they prefer boundaries and 'rules' which, to a degree, keep them safe. Knowing about something gives us a measure of control, otherwise we could be in a limbo where anything can happen.

One nine-year-old girl, who has to give herself two diabetes injections every day, commented: 'At first I didn't like it; now I'm used to it.'

A thirteen year old girl said, 'it isn't businesslike not to tell us', while an eleven year old boy, speaking of injections said, 'It's only a two-second hurt'. A seven year old thought that if he could be told ahead about injections he'd be 'given the time to get ready for it'.

What is very clear is that the younger the child, the greater the *outward* show of distress. Under sixes are still not always told about injections but what has to be avoided is a 'blanket approach' to all children, because each child is an individual.

If your child is to have treatment that may be frightening or painful then naturally you'll be distressed and may feel that you can't cope with being with him at the time. A doctor or nurse will be able to see how worried you are and will be able to lessen your fears by explaining in advance what's going to happen. Parents do not want to be fobbed off with glib explanations. They are grateful when doctors are honest with them.

There's no doubt that having a parent present helps the child but if you feel you'll only upset your child even more, then you could ask if you can sit behind a curtain and hold his hand.

Children are often frightened of (among other things):

injections
giving blood samples
being tied down
X ray machines (in case they fall on them)
machines that take plaster casts off
the overwhelming size of equipment.

NINE

Operations

The doctor and ward staff will explain operating day procedure to you and help you prepare your child for what's going to happen.

Usually a few simple explanations will satisfy a young child. You should tell him that he may be asked to wear different clothes (see opposite), he may have a little prick in his hand, or be asked to drink a special medicine, then he'll go for a ride on a trolley (see page 50), where a doctor will help him to have a special sleep.

When he wakes up he'll be back in his own bed and you will be sitting there waiting for him. He may feel a bit sore but he'll know it's the beginning of getting well enough to go home.

Routines vary from hospital to hospital, however. Some issue leaflets about what will happen and show photographs and videos and a play specialist may go through the routine with the child. He will explain what's going to happen, perhaps put a plaster on Ted, show an anaesthetising mask ('like a space-man wears'), and the cap and mask that theatre staff wear, and so on. The anaesthetist may also come to see the child so that he's not a stranger the next day.

You should make every effort to be with your child on operating day even if previously you haven't been able to visit as regularly as you would have liked, owing to other commitments. If you really can't be there then try to arrange for someone else to go whom the child knows and trusts.

On the whole, the younger the child, the greater his distress at being in hospital. This is one of the reasons why, if at all possible, operations on a child are delayed until he is over four years.

The likely routine on operating day

Nothing by mouth

Anyone undergoing surgery has to go without food for a varying number of hours. Don't give the child anything to eat – there should be a NOTHING BY MOUTH note pinned to the bed or his nightclothes.

Operating gown

He'll be asked, probably, to have a bath and then to put on an operating gown which fastens down the back. Some children object strongly to wearing such gowns (which must be made of cotton because of the danger of static or gases in operating areas.) He may be allowed to go to the theatre in a loose nightshirt or his underpants. Maybe you could get him used to the idea of a button-down-the-back nightshirt before? Make one for Ted too.

Pre-med

He'll probably be given a pre-med in his own bed in the ward. It could be medicine or an injection but either way it will make him feel contented and drowsy.

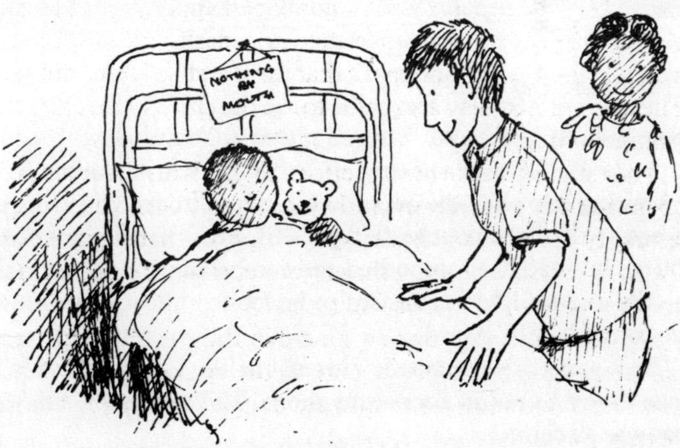

Going to the theatre

He may be wheeled to the theatre but being on the trolley worries some children. If they are small enough they could be carried by you or a porter.

Anaesthetic room

Some hospitals will let you go into the anaesthetic room – ask the previous day if you may do so. You should leave the room – without fuss – when you are asked.

If you are not going to the anaesthetic room, ask the staff when is the best moment to leave your child. One suggestion is to go when the child is still in his own bed but possibly drowsy from a pre-med. This way, you could part from him while he is still in familiar surroundings. You could then wait out of his sight but near at hand in case he wants you for a bit longer.

Recovery room

When the operation is over he will be brought into the recovery room for a while before being taken back to the ward. You should sit beside him – he may be restless at first but then will go into a more peaceful sleep. Don't try to wake him: sit quietly (have a doze yourself if you can) until he wakes naturally. Don't give him anything to eat or drink until a nurse says you can.

'I'm not *me* any more!'

James, eight years old, was admitted to hospital with acute appendicitis. The idea of staying 'overnight' thrilled him.

Visiting him after the operation, he was discovered sitting up in bed with a face puce with rage. His hair – usually abundant and curly – had been smoothed and combed down, parted in the middle and sculpted to his scalp: he looked like a scaled-down version of Noel Coward.

'*Look* at me!' he exploded. 'Just *look* at me. Look what they've done to my *hair*! I'm not *me* any more. The operation? Oh yes, that was all right.'

A child's possessions and his appearance give him self-respect. Take them away and you take away some of his identity, and his dignity. James looked silly, and he knew it. He'd lost himself. Recombing his hair into its usual tousled disarray probably did as much for his recovery as a bucketload of pills.

If your child has to be undressed when he goes into hospital, make sure he's in his own pyjamas and slippers but also that you leave his own outer clothes folded into his locker.

They are not just a reassurance that he's still 'me', that he hasn't been taken over by this strange machine they call a hospital: they're a good-luck talisman, an insurance that he will be going home one day. A proof of his independence.

'Supposing I can't stay with my child in hospital? I have other children at home – other commitments.'

To some extent your child will already be used to sharing you although of course being ill will probably make him want more attention from you.

Explain why you can't be with him all the time and assure him that you'll always come when you can.

Don't try to sneak away: always play fair and say that you're going but tell him when you'll be back and then always keep to that promise.

Talk about what you're doing when you're not with him. He will want to hear about the usual routine of your life and the family. 'I went shopping this morning' or 'I had to work but Grandma is meeting the others from school and giving them tea so that's why I can stay longer with you.'

He will be used to these routines and won't be disturbed if you let him know they're still going on.

If he seems unduly upset, talk to the nurse in charge and ask if there's any way you can do anything differently. She will be very experienced and may have all sorts of suggestions that will help. She may be able to arrange for one nurse to 'special' the child so that he has one ally he feels really belongs to him.

If possible, arrange for other visitors – friends, relations, older children. Hopefully the child's father will be taking regular turns.

Other mothers who are able to stay with their children will almost certainly include your child in their games, stories and play, especially if you explain the situation to them.

Sending cards, messages, bringing drawings from the other children are all ways of keeping in touch and beating any feelings of neglect.

You could leave a little parcel to be opened when the other mothers come and you can't.

Some districts have a 'good neighbour' scheme whose members will visit if needed. Ask the nurse in charge, the hospital Social Worker, your Health Visitor or local clinic if there's anything like that in your area.

The local branch of NAWCH will almost certainly be able to give you details or addresses: possibly they will have their own 'pool' of volunteers.

The chances are that it's the parents with young children who will be most tied and who may be unable to visit as frequently as they'd like. Older people are likely to have more time: some hospitals operate a kind of 'renta-a-gran' scheme where older people will come in and visit children.

If there's an operation or special treatment to be faced

It really is important that you should be there. Just enlist everyone you can to make that possible: not just to be there

when he goes for the operation but also to be there when he wakes up.

And what about you?

Your health is an insurance for all the family. It may seem impossible, with all these extra demands on your time and your energy, to look after yourself as well, but you must.

Accept whatever help you're offered, from giving the children their meals, bringing them back from school, to babysitting and visiting hospital in your place.

Don't neglect your own meals and rest whenever you can, even if it's at unconventional hours, such as dozing by the bedside when your child is asleep.

It is often when the time of immediate stress has passed that the reaction of tiredness sets in. If a child has been ill and in hospital, there is often extra work to do when he gets home. You may not have to make the journeys to visit him, but there could be more nursing for you to cope with, and extra demands from a convalescent child.

TEN

Food and fads

Nurse to visiting mother

'Matthew wouldn't eat any of his dinner today. He cried and cried. We couldn't understand why he didn't like it. Usually he really enjoys his dinners.'

Child, afterwards, to mother

'How could I? How could I? They said it was *braised kittens!* How could I eat dear little cooked kittens?'

It was, in fact, braised kidneys for dinner that day. Sometimes it's best not to go into details about ingredients: how many times have you disguised a disliked food in another current favourite?

Mealtimes

Mealtimes in a children's ward can be a real opportunity for visiting parents to help and feel they are being of use. They can probably also help with one or two other children, not just their own. Nurses just don't always have the time to sit and help children with their food which is where the parents come in.

Food is immensely important to young children. It's not only that they enjoy the actual food but the whole ritual of shopping, preparing, cooking and then sitting down to a meal is part of the pattern of their days.

Even a young toddler senses the knowledge of its importance when he uses it as a 'weapon' – refusing food he's decided to 'go off' for the day! If he uses the same tactics in hospital it may have the same effect – drawing attention to himself and making him feel important.

But, that ploy apart, there are several other reasons why

mealtimes in hospital could become a time of stress for a young child instead of being the enjoyable communal affair it's meant to be.

The likes and dislikes of the under-fives will have been formed by the food he's been given at home. Hospital food is almost certain to be different in some respects. Perhaps he'll eat with relish everything put in front of him: perhaps he'll play about with it and not get much down: perhaps he'll refuse in no uncertain terms. He may even misunderstand what it's all about, like the small boy asked, as he thought, to eat kittnes . . .

But there are other ways mealtimes in hospital can upset a child and here are some of them:

1. The portions offered are too large.
2. The food is unfamiliar.
3. The food is presented differently from home.
4. The atmosphere is too noisy, not relaxed.
5. The child takes so long to eat, the food gets cold and unappetising.
6. The child senses that he's being hurried and becomes anxious.

The portions offered are too large

Some hospitals 'plate' the meals – that is, portions are put on to plates in the kitchens and sent up to the wards. Other kitchens send up heated trolleys and meals are served individually in the wards. If the latter happens, then it's easier to make the portions small.

Children are very easily daunted by being presented with a mass of food they're expected to get through. Mothers could help by putting some of the food on to other plates and saving it for second helpings, if needed.

The food is unfamiliar

It's almost standard practice in hospitals today to give a choice of meals and children love the idea of 'a menu' and being in control. However, in the event, they may not always want what they've chosen!

Dieticians take trouble to give children the food they are probably used to at home – fish fingers, beefburgers, baked beans, jacket potatoes, jellies, and so on. If your child is really refusing food to such an extent that it's hindering his progress and making him unhappy then talk to the staff nurse and ask if there are ways you can help. This could be by giving her a list of his likes and dislikes, bringing in food, or preparing it yourself on the premises. (see Specialist diets on page 57).

The food is presented differently

Young babies are probably used to prepared or tinned food and will not usually make much fuss about taking what's offered them.

It's when you get into the mashed/chopped/cut-up stage that it may be difficult. If toddlers are used to mashed food, they may find they can't cope with chopped food: if they're used to chopped, then maybe they can't cope with unchopped or cut-up food. Mothers can become the mashers, choppers, cutters-up of the ward.

Children may also not be able to cope with the cutlery provided. There would be an advantage in bringing in the child's own familiar spoon, fork or pusher – whatever he's used to at home – as well as a familiar plate or dish or cup if he's been used to having his own.

The atmosphere is not relaxed

Small tables and chairs, sitting round as a family, being helped on with bibs and aprons, a general air of anticipation – all these will help to make small children feel at ease and able to join in.

Children having meals in bed may need special help with getting the food in the right place.

The child takes so long to eat that food gets cold

Some children take a terribly long time to get the food down: mothers will be used to the patience demanded, even if every mouthful needs to be accompanied by:

'Through the teeth
Past the gums
Look out, stomach
Here it comes!'

Putting the plate in a baby plate-warmer, or a dish of warm water, could help keep the food palatable. Reading a story to the table while the food's going in also helps, if the ward sister approves.

The child senses he's being hurried

He won't feel pressured, if he can be individually helped in a relaxed and friendly way.

Specialist diets

All hospital kitchens can provide for vegetarian diets but you'll need to tell the sister in charge when your child is admitted that he is vegetarian.

You'll also have to tell her if your child has a specialist diet, such as Muslim or Kosher. Usually hospitals can make provision for this, but if not, you'll need to discuss with the hospital what's best to do.

You could either bring in the food yourself or there may be a kitchen attached to the ward where you could cook or heat through small portions. Whether that's possible depends of course on the facilities available – and how many mothers have the same idea and want to cook at the same time. As always, it's a question of co-operating with the ward staff and trying to help and not get in their way.

Although there may be a few problems over food as listed above, they need not be exaggerated because all children love to join in and feel they 'belong'. You may in fact be surprised to find your fussy eater tucking in to all sorts of things he wouldn't touch at home simply because he's 'one of the gang'.

We also have to remember that the child wouldn't be in hospital if there weren't something amiss with his health – it may only be a very slight and passing indisposition but it's only understandable if he regresses a little into younger ways – and making a fuss about food may be one of them.

Two important points

1. From the nursing point of view it may be very important to keep a strict record of how much food a child has eaten. If this is so, then you could help by keeping the record. You naturally wouldn't be tempted to slip him the odd titbit and not record it.

That's not as unusual a danger as it might appear, because giving food is an expression of love. Parents want to do something for their sick child and often the only way they feel they can express that need is by giving food. So, if you aren't allowed to give food, then don't.

Remember, too, how hard it would be if a visiting brother or sister spent the time chewing his way through a bag of crisps, eyed by miserable glances from the bed. If the sick child can't eat, no one eats – at least, not in sight.

2. Whatever you do, don't give your child any snacks or titbits if he's to have an operation, X-ray or certain tests. Watch out for

the notice NOTHING BY MOUTH which would be pinned to his pyjamas or his bedrail. If there's no notice but you think there's a possibility of some treatment like that then always ask to make sure.

If you have, innocently, given him something to eat then you'll have to own up. Eating or drinking too near some procedures may mean having to delay them.

The same applies when a child is coming round from an anaesthetic: he may be thirsty and ask for a drink – but check first because there's a time limit before which he shouldn't be given anything.

ELEVEN

Play in hospitals

Not all hospitals have play specialists as members of the children's ward team nor adequately staffed playrooms but, because the importance of play in a child's development is now recognised, an increasing number do. There's certain to be some provision for play in your child's hospital and your help there is sure to be appreciated.

We all know that children learn through play but play does more than teach children about objects – weight, texture, abilities – and so on: it can soothe or stimulate, release tensions or allow them to express their feelings when they cannot do so in words or don't even realise they need to do so.

We take a great deal of trouble in providing the 'right' toys for our child's developing abilities, progressing through bricks to jig-saws and so on. Instinctively we know when a child wants his cuddly toy for comfort or a noisy toy when he wants to let off steam.

Interpreting play

A play specialist is trained to take this understanding deeper. She is able to interpret what the child is expressing through play and provide the right kind of stimulus for him. She can explain this to the nursing staff and to the parents.

Older children can put their fears and feelings into words: often a small child can only express himself through his play, (e.g. throwing Ted against the wall could mean anger) . . . We interpret that without difficulty but some feelings are rather more hidden than that.

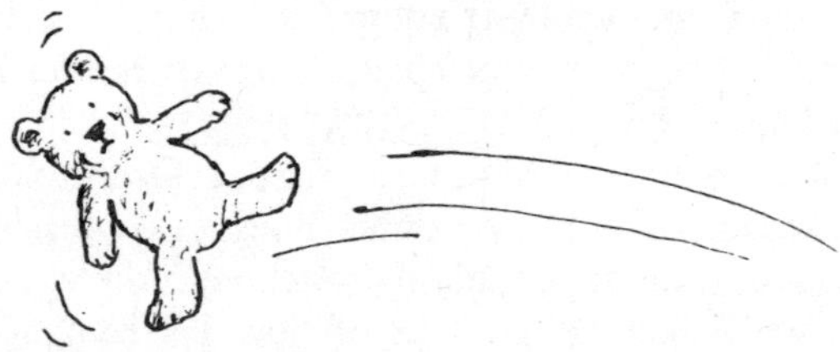

Explaining treatment through play

A play leader will, if appropriate, explain the treatment that a child is to have by letting him play with the anaesthetising mask, send his space man toy into 'special sleep', put on splints, bandage, give injections, administer pills and so on. All this will help your child to be familiar with what is happening to him or is going to happen.

Relaxing

The playroom is where a child can relax. A very sick child, too tense to sleep in the ward, has been known to drop off peacefully when his bed has been moved into the playroom.

Play allows a child to join in with others or be an individual. A play specialist will see that the children under her care get the appropriate opportunities. Many of their activities can be the

same as those they enjoy at home – painting, building, cutting out, etc., but some may be specially structured for the child's specific needs.

One activity that could be encouraged is for the older child to make a scrapbook or project of his illness or conditions: many a child has returned triumphantly to school complete with X-ray plates and a detailed account of how his broken limb was mended. Telling his class about it is therapeutic for him and informative for his friends.

Charts that show how circulation flows, how an X-ray machine works and other aspects of a hospital stay could come into the playroom or into the teaching sessions. 'To be informed is to be in control'.

What sorts of toys?

You may be surprised at the variety of things a good playroom will have – not just clean books and playthings, but pets and

'mucky' play things. A waterproof sheet on the bed, if the child is bedbound, lets a child play with sand or water in a tray, while small pets – guinea pigs, rabbits, fish – can all be kept indoors and give comfort and companionship.

TWELVE

Older children and adolescents

As far as hospital accommodation is concerned, a child may be regarded as an adult. That means he could be admitted to an adult ward where he is likely to be among middle-aged and elderly patients.

It doesn't often happen to a young child but, technically, it could. It's more likely to happen to the twelve, thirteen year olds and upwards, and, while admittedly the undiluted company of young babies in a children's ward could be boring for an adolescent, the all-day and all-night company of elderly people, some of them with distressing complaints or undergoing extreme treatment, could be very upsetting – and cause great stress.

We all need a nucleus of our own age group as companions and models against whom to a degree we 'pace' ourselves. This is particularly true of young people who are already coping with unexpected emotions and worries, moving often on a see-saw between the depths and the heights.

An adolescent is in limbo land, old enough to understand the nature of his illness and its outcome but still possibly with only partly-understood knowledge and information as sketchy as his imagination is fertile.

If you have an adolescent to be admitted to hospital ask if he can be put in a ward with others of his age. When there's no room for this he could perhaps be put in a side ward, or near others of similar age who can sometimes be screened off from the main ward, whether that's adult or children's.

Young people need privacy and also the chance to make a noise. It's a time, too, when they are particularly aware of their appearance and concerned about their body – and they're usually a lot more embarrassed about treatments than adults.

Ideally, staff should be trained in the psychological care of adolescents who need not only the dignity of privacy but also the opportunity to talk about their fears and anxieties. They have the right to know about their illness and take part in planning for its care, but to be able to express all these thoughts and emotions they may need the sympathetic encouragement of trained counsellors and psychologists to whom it is often easier to talk than to confide in members of one's own family.

If you think your adolescent is worried then ask if such a counsellor is available – it could be that the chaplain fills this place and is trained to talk to young people.

Dr Dermod MacCarthy, whose lifelong interest has been the understanding of the sick child and his parents, has written:

'The largest single measure for preservation of emotional well-being in the older child in hospital is the unhurried explanation of all unfamiliar or painful procedures whether this appears necessary or not.'

He has also written that there should be no teaching of

medical students or discussion round the bed of an older child. These could take place elsewhere.

'I was frightened all the time I was there' wrote an adolescent after a stay in hospital. Don't think that your adolescent won't need support on the day of an operation. You may have to take your cue from your own child because some, although wanting that support, may be inhibited about making themselves look 'sissies' in front of their friends. Ask the sister in charge what she advises.

Education in hospital

Continuing education is not only necessary to your child's future but it also gives a structure to the day and brings some normality into hospital life. There is also the stimulus it provides.

Legally, children in hospital have a right to the provision of education suitable to their abilities so if you think that isn't being provided ask sister or your social worker what provision is available. There should be a teacher on the staff seconded by the Local Education Authority, with whom responsibility for providing education in hospital rests.

You could find out whether your child's school would lend books, correct work and visit if needed. Providing a radio or portable television for the child's own use for school programmes might be possible – and also there should be the opportunity for uninterrupted study.

If possible, encourage your child's schoolfriends to visit, as well as any brothers or sisters in the family: these links with home add enormously to a patient's morale and the chat and gossip of friends does a lot to lift the spirits.

Some children worry that they're falling behind with school work, particularly if there's an exam looming. Others will rejoice in the opportunity! Only you will know into which category your child falls and how to deal with it. Too much emphasis on 'keeping up your school work' could cause more stress in an already worried child.

A hospital stay is unlikely to cause the after effects in an older child that it might in a younger: their greater maturity and independence helps them to survive the experience without long-term effects. Adolescents often become more mature and cooperative after a hospital stay.

THIRTEEN

Babies needing special care

A small proportion of new babies, whether they've been born in hospital or at home, need to be taken into a Special Care Baby Unit, perhaps because they are premature, or need to put on weight, or have some specific condition that needs hospital treatment.

If that should happen to your baby, you'll find that you are expected to stay in hospital with your baby for as long as is appropriate. Your bed may be beside the cot or nearby. Some units encourage fathers to stay. Almost all allow unrestricted visiting by day or night: many let other children and grandparents visit as well.

The Special Care Baby Unit may be at some distance from your home because not all hospitals have the same facilities. It can make visiting and travel difficult so it's best to talk to the staff about arrangements. You'll probably find that they encourage you to go out for walks, a meal, visit friends and so on as a long stay without a great deal to do can be depressing.

The technical equipment of a special care unit can be daunting in its size and complexity. Nursing staff will take care to explain the functions of the different pieces of machinery and you'll soon find that you'll lose your apprehension in admiration of the skill of their design and the scope of their functions.

Don't forget if you have other children visiting that they, too, may find the atmosphere overwhelming so take the trouble beforehand to explain what it will be like.

When your baby is small – and probably in an incubator – you may wonder if you're doing any good by staying at the hospital and wonder whether there could be any rapport between you and such a tiny creature. But there's no doubt that talking, feeding, stroking and cuddling your baby – when it's

permissible – all help towards giving him comfort and support. And it helps you too.

Some units encourage mothers to change nappies, help with special feeding, insert feeding tubes and generally take on some of the nursing care.

If you have other children you may think your place would be better with them, than in the hospital. Talk to the sister or the doctor in charge – they'll advise you what is best. Staff in special care baby units all have a particular interest and experience in caring for small babies and are also trained in understanding the needs of parents at such times. There is usually a larger proportion of staff to patients, too, so there's nearly always someone around to talk to.

Doctors are sometimes accused of being 'brutally honest' in telling parents about the chances and conditions of their sick babies and children but on reflection all parents appreciate this and understand that doctors, too, have great concern for the children in their care.

FOURTEEN

The family at home

A sick child affects the whole family – particularly if he is not an only child.

Even if there aren't other children, a child in hospital can disrupt a marriage. There's the extra work, the worry, interrupted schedules, usually weariness associated with to-ing and fro-ing to the hospital and possibly the absence of one partner who is staying in hospital overnight.

If all this has to be fitted in with the practicalities of a smooth-running home – cleaning, paying bills, washing, shopping and cooking – then the situation can become nightmarish.

Here are a few suggestions that might help:

1. Spend some of the time while you're at the hospital in making methodical lists, covering ideas such as:

   Could someone collect a weekly wash, take it to the laundrette and return it? Friends are often willing to take on one job and do it conscientiously but can't commit themselves to more than that.

   Could someone do a weekly shop, with you providing a basic list? Or could you bulk buy? Bought frozen meals, stored in the freezer are also an invaluable stand-by.

   Write a menu for the week, geared to your shopping list. It could be for the partner at home or for shared meals if you're both at home together sometimes.

2. Make a box, or designate a place, for all the letters, bills, notices etc. so they don't get spread over the house and lost. You could probably answer some of them while you're at the hospital. Other children in the family add to these preoccupations and make it even more necessary to be as methodical as possible.

3. Enlist friends, relatives, the school, your Health Visitor, Home Help, Childminders, your GP, teachers and your

clergyman, if appropriate, to help. Don't suffer alone or in silence. If there's help around, take it.

4. By dividing up the children's material needs – school clothes, homework, food, and so on, – you can give out responsibilities at home in different directions.

If they're old enough, children like to have their own job: a rota on the wall has enormous attractions, particularly if the eldest appoints himself as foreman and sees there's no strike action.

But practicalities apart, children at home can suffer a great deal from unjustified feelings of guilt: that somehow the child in hospital is ill through something they've done. They can also be frightened that they may get the same complaint.

Point out that there are plenty of other children in the school, or in the street, who haven't got it so why should they? Anticipate any feelings of guilt by explaining that the invalid was unlucky enough to come up against germs (for instance) when he couldn't cope with them but that doesn't mean anyone else is going to.

When you are able to be at home, try and give your whole attention to the needs of the others in the family. Listen to what's happening at school, praise schoolwork and homework, and perhaps arrange 'treats' even if it's something simple like shopping for new shoes, talking about a holiday or what you'll do when everything's back to normal.

Try and arrange for someone else to take over the hospital

visiting occasionally so that you have time with your partner alone, or with him and the family.

Keep the children in touch with each other by taking messages back and forwards, sending cards and drawings – telling each of the doings of the other so that you are a bridge between the two worlds.

If the children are an appropriate age, make a scrapbook to explain what's happening in hospital and how soon the sick child will be home.

Building up children's health in times of stress is very important, so whenever you can, make sure they eat properly and have adequate rest as well as periods of 'togetherness' and fun.

Stress that all this is a temporary affair: planning something special to happen after you're all back to normal is a great help. It can be something quite simple like a visit, or a new possession or activity.

If conditions are suitable, take one or more of the children to visit the child in hospital: it will help them all.

FIFTEEN

Convalescence

Many parents notice, once their child has been discharged and is home again, that he has in some way 'changed'. There are well-known behaviour incidents – reversion to babyish habits, thumb-sucking, losing bladder control, needing his mother in sight all the time, perhaps head-banging, rocking or masturbation.

It's not difficult to understand, because to a degree when we're not well we want to draw a bit of attention to ourselves – and to 'baby' ourselves with extra comforts. So a child who behaves like this is partly seeking a little more attention and partly growing up again – he needs time to catch up to where he left off.

Don't scold him about such things as thumb sucking or bed-wetting: try to anticipate the latter as you did when he was being toilet trained but take it all as cheerfully and matter-of-factly as possible. He needs more cuddling and attention, although if there are other children in the family try not to give so much attention to the returned warrior that the others get left out.

Remember, too, that children in hospital are seldom bored. They have company all the time, things going on, things to watch: '*even very ill children*', Dr Hugh Jolly used to say, '*play with their eyes*'. You have only to watch a sick child following movements going on and 'joining in' to know how true that is.

So home can be a bit boring, back in the old routine. Try to involve the child as much as possible so that you do things together – sorting out the washing, putting the cutlery away, making the shopping list – as well as joining in his hobbies, such as watching a television programme together, reading stories, or making a scrapbook.

Avoid battles and confrontations as you would have done while he was being 'trained', and don't put adverse reactions down to naughtiness.

He may want to be taken up to bed at night, sat by until he's asleep, have a nightlight or say he wants to eat with his fingers. Keep calm, ignore it if possible, and remember that all tunnels have light at the end.

More serious are reactions such as, for example, nightmares, fear of scissors (which could bring back unpleasant memories of hospital treatment), loss of bowel control or coming into your bed at night. They can be time-consuming and patience-trying but they are not after all very difficult to understand. Your child has been through an experience that even adults find disturbing; making battles out of the problems makes them into double problems – the original one and your reaction to it.

What is important is to let the child know that you're 'on his side' and that you're not comparing him with other children to his disadvantage. What a child may have learnt through a hospital stay is that the world isn't entirely safe, and that parents can't always protect him from unpleasant things. It's an enormously frightening discovery and he needs time to come to terms with it. It's one of the biggest steps towards growing up.

Some children show their fear and resentment at having a stay in hospital by aggression towards other children, their possessions or their parents – usually the mother. There's a thin line to be drawn between quietly understanding the behaviour and condoning it. If the child is old enough you could say, 'I know you feel angry about things – we all do, sometimes. But we do love you very much so let's do something about all these nasty feelings.'

Six-year-old James habitually upset his three younger sisters every afternoon when he came home from school. 'If you feel ratty,' his mother suggested, 'because you've had to put up with people telling *you* what to do all day, why don't you tell somebody here what to do?'

'Like?' asked James.

'Weeds in the garden,' she suggested, with an eye to the main chance. 'Tell them to go!'

He took the bait, attacked the weeds with the ferocity of a Kung Fu fanatic and peace reigned among his sisters. Except, when they saw how much he enjoyed weeding, they did it too . . . There were renewed squalls. 'What about sorting out the lumps of coal?' suggested his mother wearily.

But of course for more peaceful therapy there is nothing like making a story out of the child's experiences. Go back to

Christopher's story about his tests for deafness: he not only taught us so much but he also explained it to himself. Making a story book about the child's stay in hospital – drawing nurse, putting in sentences or drawings at his suggestions – will often 'fix' the incidents in his mind and set him free from the threat by allowing him to 'talk out' his fears and put them into perspective.

SIXTEEN

Fares and finances

Visiting a child in hospital inevitably involves extra expense, the most obvious being the cost of fares to and from the hospital.

If your home is near the hospital these may not be excessive but sometimes a child has to be treated in a specialist unit which may be some miles away. This is because the equipment in such units is very expensive, and it has to serve a large area.

One family, whose seven year old son had to be treated in a unit eighty miles from their home, estimated that in two years they travelled sixteen to twenty thousand miles and spent between five and six thousand pounds in fares.

Families on Income Support can claim a refund of all or part of their fares from the DHSS. There is no fixed entitlement and today it will be a discretionary grant from the Social Fund. Many parents who could claim, don't bother to do so, saying it's 'too much hassle' but it's surely worth making at least one or two personal (or phone) calls to your local Social Services office. Maybe, if you are already too occupied with your child as it is, a friend could make the preliminary enquiries for you.

You may also be entitled to local authority assistance – such as a Home Help – with your other children. You might also be able to claim paid leave from your place of work.

The social worker at the hospital or your local DHSS office will be able to advise you about these claims.

The hospital social worker will also probably have a fund available for help with fares – but she has to get the money from somewhere and this is where voluntary efforts come in.

Many NAWCH branches raise money for their local hospitals to help with parents' needs and so also may other voluntary societies such as 'Friends of the Hospital'.

Volunteers also run ferrying services for parents and patients who need to go to the hospital. The South Manchester branch of NAWCH, for instance, runs a computer-based transport scheme and others run rotas for local transport – although more drivers are always needed.

Quite often, your Health Visitor will know of resources available or may be able to put you in touch with someone who could help. Your doctor may also have details of what facilities there are in your area.

Some of the ways in which voluntary workers can help children in hospital

1. Staff a playgroup or provide childminding in Outpatients, Ante-natal or Accident and Emergency departments.
2. Finance a playleader either for those areas in (1) or for a ward.
3. Provide plants, posters, toys, books etc. for the above departments or at Ante-natal clinics.
4. Provide Christmas stockings, a Christmas tree or a Father Christmas to distribute the presents.
5. Assist with hospital radio programmes.
6. Visit children who don't have regular visitors – after liaison with the Sister in charge or social worker.
7. Ferry parents to and from hospital, or organise rotas for this.
8. Produce a newsletter and/or distribute NAWCH leaflets, colouring books etc.
9. Seek sponsorship from local firms for specific needs in the hospital (talk to the hospital staff about this first).

SEVENTEEN

Accidents and First Aid

Accidents

We haven't tried to deal in detail with accidents in this book but here are a few pointers which are worth considering as they may help to avoid a hospital visit.

1. Most accidents to young children take place in the home. The kitchen is the most dangerous place.

2. Most accidents in the home take place between 8 to 9 a.m. and 5 to 7 p.m., which are the times when there's most hurry and stress in the majority of homes.

For example, *scalds* most frequently happen to the under-4s, through drinking from too-hot containers, having hot contents spilled on them, pulling over saucepans or kettles, and being put in too-hot bath water. (See also page 81).

3. 'Get rid of your coffee table', is the advice of one most experienced nurse. 'Things on it are too accessible – cigarette stubs left in ash-trays, peanuts which can cause suffocation if inhaled, tea and coffee trays are too easy to reach. I have nursed a badly scalded child who drank from the teapot . . . I also don't like baby-walkers if they are allowed to lead toddlers into situations they can't cope with – I've known more than one tipped into a fire . . .'

First Aid

Here's a very simple guide to the first-aid you may need in an emergency. It has been kept to the basics so that they are easy to remember.

Breaks

Try not to move the child, unless it's necessary, if you think he has broken a limb. If you *have* to move him, be very gentle, particularly if you think he may have injured his neck or spine. If you think he's broken a leg, tie the injured limb very gently to the uninjured one, putting padding in between his legs. Put an injured arm in a sling or support.

Burns

Put the burn in cold water, or under a running cold-water tap, for at least ten minutes. This reduces surface heat. Take off anything tight – rings, belts, etc. – as burnt skin can swell, but if burnt clothes are stuck to the skin, don't try to take them off.

Cover the burn with a clean, non-fluffy cloth which will cut down the risk of infection. Call an ambulance or take the child to hospital for anything other than a very small burn.

Choking

If you can reach the object, then do so. If not, turn the child upside down, holding him by the legs, and slap smartly between the shoulder blades. If nothing happens, try again. If the object isn't dislodged, as a last resort give a sharp, short squeeze to the tummy, with the child in an *upright* position.

Cuts

Press firmly on the wound with your fingers or a pad of clean cloth until the bleeding stops. Try to press the edges of the wound together. If appropriate, lay the child down and raise the injured limb – *but not if you think it may be broken.* Cover the wound with a clean dressing and call an ambulance.

Poisoning

1. *Pills and medicines*

Check first that your child really has swallowed pills or medicine. If you're certain, take him straight to your doctor or hospital, taking with you the container and a sample of whatever has been swallowed. Do not give salt and water.

2. *Household and garden chemicals*
Give a glass of milk to drink, or water if there's no milk. This will dilute the poison. Take the child immediately to your doctor or hospital and take a sample of whatever you think has been swallowed.

Scalds

Put the scald at once in cold water or under running cold water for at least ten minutes. Take off any clothes covering the scald and remove anything tight, e.g. rings or belts, as scalded skin can swell. Cover with a clean non-fluffy cloth and call for an ambulance or take the child to hospital.

Shock

If pale and unwell after an accident, make the child lie down. Keep him warmly covered but don't make him too hot. If a lot of blood has been lost, raise the legs and keep the head down but *not* if you think there might be a head injury or broken leg.

Suffocation

Take away whatever has caused the suffocation and give mouth-to-mouth resuscitation, (see page 82).

Your first aid kit

This should contain:

- Box of adhesive dressings
- Box of sterile gauze dressings
- 2 cotton bandages
- 2 crepe bandages
- clean cotton cloth (to use as sling or dressing for burn or scald)
- Cotton wool for padding
- Blunt ended scissors
- Safety pins and adhesive tape
- antiseptic cream
- Telephone numbers, as suggested on page 30

Mouth to mouth resusciation

1. Clear the child's mouth of dirt, vomit etc.
2. Bend the head back and push the jaw upwards to lift the tongue off the back of the throat.
3. Squeeze the nostrils together, put your mouth over the child's mouth and blow gently. See the chest rise.
4. Take your mouth away and let the chest fall.
5. Repeat this about fifteen times a minute.
6. When the child begins to breathe, place the child in the recovery position (see page 83).
7. If you think the heart has stopped (the child may be very pale or a blue/grey colour) give heart massage as well as mouth to mouth resuscitation.

Heart massage

Lay the child on his back on the floor. Kneel to one side. Press the lower half of the child's breast bone (moderate pressure for a young child, less still for a baby). Press about every second for a child, quicker for a baby. Use your thumb when massaging a baby – it regulates itself and is not too heavy. Repeat about five times, then stop and give resuscitation. If another person is with you, one can do the breathing and one the massage, stopping every five seconds to let the other fill up the child's lungs.

When the heart starts beating, keep on with the resuscitation until the breathing starts. Then place in the recovery position (see below).

Recovery position

Turn the child half-way on to his front, the underneath arm stretched behind and the upper arm bent in front. Bend the upper leg to right angles with the body. The face should be towards the ground with the neck back so that the tongue falls forward and the child can breathe.

Never leave an unconscious child alone.

Dial 999 for an ambulance or ask someone else to do so.

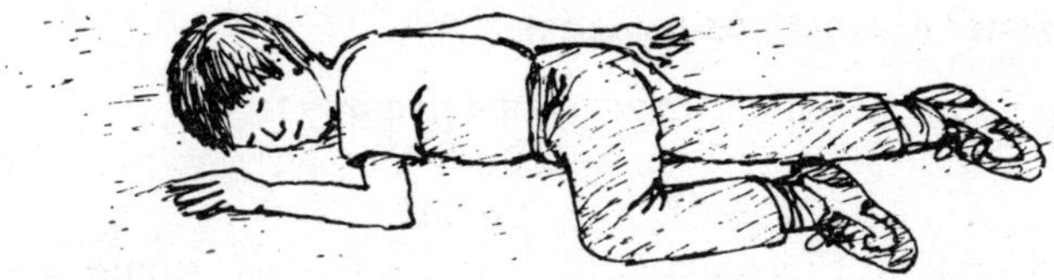

DO NOT

1. Give a child a drink or anything to eat if you think he may need an anaesthetic.
2. Put grease on any burns, or prick any blisters.
3. Move a child if you think he has broken a limb unless you have to, and then be very gentle.
4. Give a child salt and water to drink if he's swallowed *pills and medicines*.
   But it's the opposite advice if he's drunk *garden or household chemicals*: then give a drink of milk and/or plain water which will dilute the poison.
5. Panic – it's catching.

NAWCH

The National Association for the Welfare of Children in Hospital was started in 1961. NAWCH works for all children in hospital to be cared for in children's wards with specially trained staff, unrestricted visiting for their parents and accommodation for parents to stay overnight. NAWCH aims to persuade hospitals that parents have a necessary and practical part to play in the care of their sick child, and convince parents of the importance of being with their child to provide continuing love and support.

NAWCH receives a Government grant for its work and runs a national information service for those concerned with the welfare of sick children. Local NAWCH branches around the country give practical support and advice to families with a child in hospital and liaise with professionals involved in children's health care.

NAWCH produces publications for parents to help them prepare for a hospital admission for their child. A price list is available on receipt of an SAE from NAWCH, Argyle House, 29/31 Euston Road, London NW1 2SD.

If you need help or information, please contact NAWCH.

INDEX